GUIDE TO Young Rider's

Buying a Horse or Pony

Young Rider's
GUIDE TO

Buying a
Horse or
Pony

LESLEY WARD

HOWELL BOOK HOUSE
NEW YORK

All photographs were taken by the author unless otherwise credited.

Howell Book House
A Simon & Schuster Macmillan Company
1633 Broadway
New York, NY 10019

MACMILLAN is a registered trademark of Macmillan, Inc.

Library of Congress Cataloging-in-Publication Data

Ward, Lesley.
Young rider's guide to buying a horse or pony / Lesley Ward.
        p. cm.
        ISBN 0-87605-931-0
        1. Horses—Juvenile literature. 2. Horsemanship—Juvenile literature.
        3. Horses—Buying—Juvenile literature. 4. Ponies—Juvenile literature.
        [1. Horses. 2. Horsemanship. 3. Horses—Buying. 4. Ponies.] I. Title.
        SF302.W338 1996
        636.1'0029'7—dc20   96–22098
                                                                        CIP
                                                                        AC

Manufactured in the United States of America

10 9 8 7 6 5 4 3 2 1

BOOK DESIGN BY GEORGE J. MCKEON

Contents

Do you love horses? Because you are reading this book you probably do! And like many other horse-crazy people, you probably dream of having a horse or pony of your own. Well, who knows? You just might achieve that dream someday.

This book will help you to buy a first horse that is just right for you. Remember, a bad horse costs just as much as a good horse to keep, so why not make sure you buy a terrific horse in the first place? You'll be glad you made the effort.

A good first horse will be your teacher. He will help you to improve your riding skills and become a confident rider. And if he is a nice, well-mannered horse, he will quickly become your best friend.

But before you start your search for the perfect horse, you must sit down and read this book. Ask your parents to read it, too. After all, they are going to be your partners in buying a horse.

Buying a first horse isn't a simple process. The perfect horse won't just appear on your doorstep. It takes a lot of time and effort, plus some help from an experienced riding instructor. The right horse or pony is out there somewhere, he's just waiting for you to find him!

Are You Ready?

Before you begin your search for a horse, it's a good idea to ask yourself, "Am I experienced enough to look after a horse?" Be honest!

Do you know how much a horse eats every day? Do you know *what* he eats? Do you know when he needs shoes? Do you know what to do if a horse is sick? Do you know how to keep a horse healthy and fit?

You also need to be honest about your riding ability. Do you know how to start, stop, walk, trot, and canter? If you don't know the answers to these questions yet, taking lessons at a riding school is an excellent way to learn.

BEING A GOOD STUDENT

Taking regular riding lessons and working hard will show your parents that you are serious about wanting a horse. Here are some simple rules to follow:

- Arrive on time for your lessons and pay attention to the instructor.

A RIDING SCHOOL IS A GREAT PLACE TO LEARN HOW TO TAKE CARE OF A HORSE.

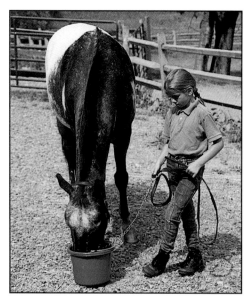

YOU NEED TO KNOW WHAT A HORSE EATS BEFORE YOU BUY ONE.

- Ask questions if you don't understand what is being taught. A good instructor will not mind explaining something twice. Tell your instructor that you want to learn all you can about horses.

- Ask if you can arrive at the barn before your lesson and watch as the horse you are going to ride is tacked up by a stable worker. After several lessons, you could volunteer to tack up the horse by yourself.

ALWAYS PAY ATTENTION TO YOUR RIDING INSTRUCTOR.

• Ask your teacher if you can stay after your lesson and help clean tack or feed the horses. She may be happy to have the extra help, and you will learn a lot about horses by just being with them.

• Go to your library and check out books on horses and riding. Trade horse books with friends, too. Read them from cover to cover. Make a special notebook and write down any interesting horse facts that you learn.

OFFER TO HELP TACK UP THE RIDING SCHOOL HORSES.

3

STAY AFTER YOUR LESSON AND LEARN HOW TO MAKE A SADDLE SHINE.

SUMMER CAMP

Many riding schools offer summer camps. If yours does, sign up! Summer camps allow you to spend all day at the barn—you'll be in horse heaven!

You'll ride once or twice every day and have horse care lessons, too. You will learn all sorts of useful things, such as the names of the different parts of a horse and the golden rules of feeding. You will also be taught how to groom and tack up a horse. These important skills will come in handy when you get a horse of your own.

At summer camp, you may be assigned one horse to look after and ride during your stay. It's just like having your own horse, and will be great experience for when you own a horse yourself! You'll also meet lots of kids who love horses as much as you do, and you will make some great friends.

WORKING STUDENTS

Once you have some experience and decide that one lesson a week isn't enough for you, find out if your school has working students. Many schools let their pupils ride in exchange for working a few hours a week. Working students usually have to muck out stables, clean saddles, or tack up horses

BE A WORKING STUDENT AND HELP BEGINNER RIDERS.

before lessons. You may be asked to help beginner students.

Being a working student will teach you a lot about horses, but make sure you know how many hours you will be expected to work. You don't want to work 100 hours for 1 measly hour of riding! Ask your parents to discuss the details with the stable manager, and ask the other helpers if they like working there before you sign up to be a working student.

LEASING A HORSE

Leasing a horse is a great way to tell if you are ready to own a horse of your own. Leasing is like renting a horse.

Sometimes an owner outgrows her horse, or for some reason can't ride him herself. She does not want to sell her friend but wants to make sure he is well cared for.

She offers the horse to a suitable person (you) who will look after him for an agreed length of time, but he still belongs to the owner. If you lease a horse, you will be responsible for paying for his feed and board.

Before you decide to lease a horse, your parents must sign a contract with the horse's owner. It should include these points:

✔ How long will the lease last?

✔ Where will the horse be kept?

SHARE A HORSE WITH A PONY PAL.

✔ What can you do with the horse? Can you take him to shows or jump him?

✔ Who is going to pay for things like vet bills and shoeing?

✔ Will the horse come with tack (a saddle, stirrups and leathers) and blankets?

SHARING A HORSE

Sometimes sharing a horse with another person is a good idea. Your instructor might know of someone who would like to share a horse. The horse's board, feed, vet, and shoeing bills are split between the two partners.

Before you think about sharing a horse, you must sit down with your potential partner and discuss your riding schedules. A horse should not be ridden too much, and it's a good idea for the two of you to ride him on different days. It's best if each partner gets three days a week.

The extra day can be a rest day for the horse.

Sharing a horse can sometimes be tricky, especially if something goes wrong, for example, the horse gets sick. You and your partner might disagree about important things, such as how much to feed the horse or whether he should be kept in a stable at night. You have to be willing to compromise, and you must realize that you might not get to ride as often as you would wish.

A HORSE THAT HAS WON LOTS OF RIBBONS MAY BE EXPENSIVE.

THE HARD FACTS ABOUT HORSE OWNERSHIP

It's a good idea to take riding lessons for about six months before you buy a horse. Ask your instructor if she thinks you are ready to be a horse owner. If she says "yes," then you need to sit down and discuss the following points with your parents:

- A horse can cost from several hundred to several thousand dollars, depending on his breeding and experience. The

A HORSE OWNER HAS TO PAY FARRIER BILLS.

7

YOUR NEW HORSE WILL NEED TACK AND GROOMING EQUIPMENT.

more ribbons he has won, the more he will cost! Do you have enough money to buy a horse that will be suitable for you?

• Once you buy a horse, the bills will start. There will be vet and feed bills. You'll have to pay a farrier to trim his feet every four to six weeks. You will also need enough money to take care of emergencies. When a horse gets sick, the vet bills can be huge!

• You'll have to buy tack and grooming equipment: a saddle, leathers, stirrups, blankets, brushes, and other supplies.

• Your horse will need a home. You must decide where he is going to live before you even start shopping for him. Do you live on a farm or have land where you can look after your-self? Is there a boarding barn nearby where you will pay someone else to care for him? Can you keep him at the rid-ing school where you have been taking lessons? You and your parents should have a clear idea of where your new horse will live and how much it will cost to feed and house him.

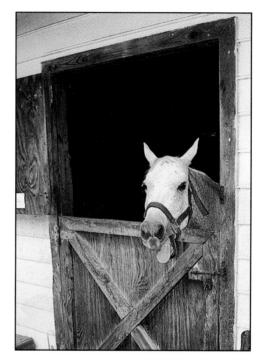

DO YOU HAVE SOMEWHERE YOU CAN KEEP A HORSE?

• Do you have enough time to spend with a horse? He will need lots of exercise and atten-tion. You must visit a pony every day to make sure he is healthy and happy.

2 Where to Look for the Perfect Horse

Always start a search by asking and listening for news of ponies or horses for sale in your area. Let everyone know that you are looking for one. Your instructor or the manager of your riding school may know of a good horse for sale.

Some of the best horses never appear in advertisements. That's because there is a line of people waiting to get their hands on them as soon as the owners think of selling!

The great thing about buying a well-known local horse is that it is easy to check up on his reputation, temperament, and health.

NEWSPAPERS

Look in the newspaper every day. Many newspapers have a "Horses and Livestock for Sale" section in the classified ads.

If you look through the ads quickly, it might seem like there are lots of great horses for sale. But beware. People are not always honest when describing the horse or pony they are

The local paper is a good place to look for a horse.

trying to sell. A horse that sounds perfect in an ad might be a disappointment when you actually meet him.

AD TALK

Remember that no one is going to say, "I want to sell a badly behaved horse that bites kids." You have to read ads carefully. Here are some terms and phrases to watch for when buying a first horse.

- **Ideal first or second horse, Pony Club/4-H pony, perfect for novice rider:** Means that he is well behaved, experienced and good for learners.

- **Good all-rounder:** Means he does flatwork, jumps and is calm on trail rides.

- **Bombproof, safe, and quiet:** Means he won't be scared by engine noises or unexpected happenings.

- **Well mannered:** Means he is well behaved and won't bully you.

- **Honest and willing:** Means he will do what he is asked and will try anything without being stubborn.

- **Good to clip/shoe/catch/trailer:** Means that he stands still when he is clipped, is well behaved for the farrier, is easily caught in the field, and steps into a horse trailer with no fuss.

    Don't respond to an ad if you see these terms and phrases.

- **Not novice ride:** Means he needs an experienced rider.

- **Green horse:** Means he is inexperienced and does not know how to do many things. He needs training.

- **Potential working hunter/show jumper:** Means you will have to train him yourself. He is still green.

CHECK THE BULLETIN BOARD AT THE TACK SHOP FOR HORSE ADS.

- **Lively, spirited, needs confident rider**: Means he is hard to control.

- **Fast:** Means he may not want to stop!

TACK SHOP BULLETIN BOARDS

Many tack shops or feed stores have bulletin boards where people post notices about horses and ponies for sale. Sometimes the tack shop owner knows the animals advertised and can give you information about them.

TAKE A SCHOOL HORSE ON A CROSS-COUNTRY RIDE BEFORE YOU BUY HIM.

Visit the store at least once a week to check for new advertisements.

RIDING SCHOOLS

A riding school favorite can be a great first horse. Schools are sometimes open to offers for their horses, but don't expect the horse to be cheap. Riding schools treasure their really well-behaved horses.

Buying a riding school horse is a terrific idea. You have already ridden the horse and get along with him. Your instructor knows him as well, and can tell if you two are going to be compatible in the long run.

But remember, some horses have a habit of changing when they are free of the indoor arena and lose the comforting nose-to-tail company of their horse

RIDING SCHOOL HORSES MAKE EXCELLENT FIRST HORSES.

PONY CLUB AND 4-H

Ask your parents to call the leaders of the local Pony Club or the 4-H. These people may know of horses that have been outgrown by their riders and are for sale. Let them know how much you have ridden and how experienced you are around horses.

PONY CLUB HORSES ARE USUALLY EXPERIENCED AND WELL BEHAVED.

pals. Try the horse outside of a lesson. Take him in a ring by himself for a schooling session to see how he behaves. Go on a trail ride with him to see if he is calm and sensible.

Horses that have participated in Pony Club and 4-H activities are likely to be well looked after and healthy. They are used to being around kids and are usually experienced all-rounders.

DEALERS

A dealer is someone who buys and sells horses and ponies for clients. He or she will find out what sort of horse you want and look for one that fits the description. Dealers will charge you for the service or take a commission—a fee—from the seller.

Ask your riding school instructor if she knows a dealer with a good reputation in your area. Honest dealers will not sell you a bad horse because it might hurt their reputation. Good dealers will offer to buy back a horse if it turns out to have problems. You can ask for a warranty on a horse—just like on a car!

A dealer might have several horses for you to try. He or she should be happy to let a vet inspect the horse and won't mind

LET YOUR NEW HORSE FIND YOU!

if you want to try the horse more than once.

Don't trust a pushy dealer who says things like, "You'll have to decide now if you want this horse because I've got another customer coming later who has offered me cash," or who tries to sell you a horse you don't like.

WANT ADS

If you can't find the horse you want, why not let him find you? Putting a "horse wanted" ad in your local newspaper or in a horse magazine lets people know that you are looking for a horse. Write your ad carefully. State the following:

- Age, size, and type of horse you want
- How much you can pay
- How far you will travel to try the horse

Remember that some people grow very attached to their horses and want them to have good homes. You may have to convince the seller that you will be a caring owner.

CHARITIES AND RESCUE CENTERS

Horse charities raise money so that they can help neglected, abused, or abandoned horses and ponies.

WHY DON'T YOU SPONSOR A HORSE AT A CHARITY FARM?

Many charities have rescue centers or farms where they take rescued horses to recover from abuse.

Often these centers nurse a horse or pony back to health and then try to find a suitable home for him. They look for someone to adopt the horse. They prefer to place a horse with experienced horse people. The charity remains the owner of the horse and checks on him regularly.

Rescued horses don't always make good first horses. Some have been mistreated and are afraid of humans, and they may kick or bite. Some have medical problems and others have never been ridden or trained properly.

Instead of adopting an abused horse, why don't you help a charity by sponsoring one? The horse remains at the rescue center and you donate a small amount of money each year and can visit him. It is unlikely that you will need to ride or groom a horse at a rescue center, but the manager will probably let you feed a carrot or apple to your adopted horse.

AUCTIONS

Don't look here! Auctions are not good places to buy a first horse unless you are with an experienced horse person.

It might seem tempting to buy a horse this way because there can be bargains at auctions. But going to an auction for a first horse is asking for trouble. You know nothing about the horses and ponies that are for sale, and it's impossible to be sure of their real age, health, experience, and ability. Small auctions rarely have a ring where you can try a horse properly, so you probably won't get much time in the saddle.

There is often a very good reason why an owner wants to get rid of a horse quickly. He might be lame, ill, or badly behaved. And some auction sales are final! You won't get your money back if you buy a bad horse.

The biggest problem with an auction is that you don't have time to think carefully. The best advice is always, "Don't rush into anything."

3 What Sort of Horse Do You Need?

Before you head out to look at potential four-legged friends, it's important that you, your parents, and your instructor think about the type of horse that will be suitable for you.

AGE OF HORSE

Many people think they should only look for a young horse, one under the age of eight. They are mistaken. Older, more experienced horses make the best first horses.

If you haven't ridden very much, a young horse can cause all sorts of problems. If he is inexperienced, or "green," he will need lots of special training.

If you are learning to ride, a young horse may take advantage of you. He may pick up bad habits, like bucking or dropping his head to eat grass. A young horse may not know how to canter on the correct lead and he may never have jumped. Wouldn't you rather have a horse that can do it all already?

A horse that is over eight will usually know how to walk, trot, and canter on command. He has probably jumped, too.

TRY TO BUY AN OLDER, MORE EXPERIENCED HORSE.

Horses can live into their twenties, so a "teenager" will probably be around for a long time.

In fact, if they have been well trained, horses in their teens are sometimes the best horses of all. They will have experienced more things than a young horse and will be calmer in stressful situations. An older horse will give you lots of confidence and make you a better rider because he already knows a lot more than you!

SIZE

If you have been taking riding lessons, you may have an idea of what size horse or pony you need. Ask your riding teacher what size she thinks is best for you. A pony measures up to 14.2 hands. Anything above this is a horse.

If you are tall, you might consider buying a small horse as your "first pony." However, a horse

Measuring Up

Do you know that ponies and horses are measured in "hands"? The height of a pony is found by taking the measurement of a straight line from the ground to the highest point of his withers, which are at the base of his neck.

A hand is equal to 4 inches, or the width of a man's hand. The name of the measurement comes from a time long ago when people used their hands to measure a horse. When you see the letters "hh" after a measurement, it means "hands high."

You must be able to tack up your horse alone. If he's so tall that you cannot put the saddle on his back or get the bridle over his ears, then he's not the horse for you.

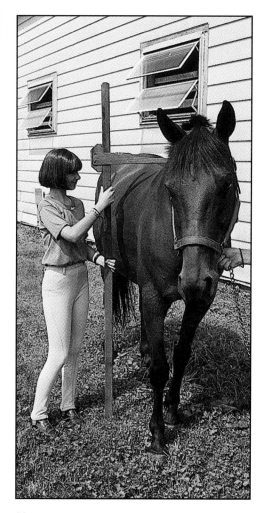

USE A MEASURING STICK TO CHECK A HORSE'S HEIGHT.

must not be too big for you. If he is too big, he could be too strong and you may not be able to stop him. If he is huge, your legs would have as much power as wet noodles on his sides. Your lower legs must reach at least halfway down the sides of a horse.

YOU MUST BE ABLE TO TACK UP YOUR NEW HORSE ALL BY YOURSELF.

You should also be able to get on him by yourself, without the help of a mounting block.

SHOWTIME

If you plan to compete with a new pony in shows that are run by the American Horse Shows Association (AHSA), his size will be important because the AHSA divides its classes by height. These are the AHSA class sizes:

- A small pony is 12.2 hh and under

- A medium pony is 12.3 to 13.2 hh

- A large pony is 13.3 to 14.2 hh

IS YOUR SHOW PONY SMALL, MEDIUM, OR LARGE?

A Perfect Fit

Here is a rough guide to horse and pony sizes (if you are of average height and build for your age):

HEIGHT OF HORSE OR PONY	APPROXIMATE AGE OF RIDER
Under 11 hands	Under 7 years
Between 11 and 12.2 hands	Between 7 and 9 years
Between 12.2 and 13.2 hands	Between 9 and 12 years
Between 13.2 and 14.2 hands	Between 12 and 14 years
Between 14.2 and 15.2 hands	Between 14 and 16 years

The people who run AHSA shows are very strict and will ask you to provide a "card of valid measurement" signed by a veterinarian.

SEX

If a horse is well behaved and nice to ride, it doesn't matter if he is a gelding (a male horse that has been neutered by a vet so he cannot father a foal) or a mare (a female). Both sexes can make excellent first horses.

A few mares can be moody and sensitive when they are "in season" (ready to mate) but this behavior only lasts a few days a

MARES CAN BE JUST AS WELL BEHAVED AS GELDINGS.

YOUR NEW HORSE MUST HAVE A FRIENDLY PERSONALITY.

month during the summer. During this time they may be touchy and try to nip you when you groom them. They may also act nasty toward other horses. But most mares in season will still do their jobs without much fuss— you may not even know they are in season.

Stallions (male horses that have not been neutered) are not suitable as first horses because they can be unpredictable. Stallions are not allowed at many 4-H and Pony Club events.

PERSONALITY

A horse's personality is very important. You want a horse that is good-tempered and friendly. A first horse should be confident and calm. When you meet him, he should have his ears forward and be interested in you.

You should be able to pet him and walk around him without him making grumpy faces and getting restless.

Avoid horses that are stubborn, high-strung, and nervous. Stay clear of horses that are bullies and barge right past you in the stable.

Even if a horse is talented, you won't enjoy him if he bites or kicks. It is almost impossible to change a horse's personality as he gets older, so don't think you will be able to make him nicer.

PRICE

An experienced horse is going to cost more than an untrained one. A horse that has won lots of ribbons in shows will cost more than one that has only trotted around the field behind his owner's house.

Horse prices vary from area to area. Ask your riding instructor how much a suitable all-rounder should cost in your area and stick to that range when looking for a horse. Watch out for "bargain" horses—they could have something physically wrong with them or have personality problems.

A well-trained show horse can cost thousands of dollars. But a first horse doesn't have to be a top-class show star. A good first horse can sometimes cost less than a thousand dollars.

COLOR

Color should be the last requirement on your list. Ignore people

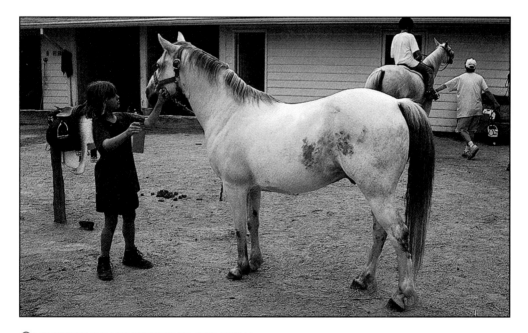

Gray ponies can be difficult to keep clean.

25

TALENTED HORSES COME IN ALL COLORS!

be important. There's no point in having a beautiful Palomino if he is naughty and you can't ride him.

Of course, some horses are a little harder to keep clean than others. Gray horses seem to attract mud and grass stains and are difficult to keep spotless. But if you are too lazy to groom your horse, maybe you shouldn't buy one!

KEEP AN OPEN MIND!

Do you have your heart set on a fancy purebred horse, or will you be open-minded and look at any horse that seems suitable? Sadly, there are very few perfect horses, so be prepared to compromise.

You might dream of having a beautiful chestnut horse with a shiny coat and a white blaze, but you should still go to look at, and ride, the fuzzy bay horse that is advertised in your local paper. Underneath that shaggy coat might be a well-behaved and talented horse that will be a loyal friend.

who spread fairy tales like "Chestnut mares are always trouble." A chestnut mare can be as good as any other horse.

If a horse is well behaved and you like him, his color should not

4 Which Breed?

A breed is a group of horses that look alike and have the same ancestors. Horses of the same breed share the same physical traits. For example, most Arabians have a "dished" face and small ears.

A purebred horse has parents that are of the same breed. Breeders take great care to match a high-quality mare to a high-quality stallion to produce a purebred foal. A **mixed breed** horse has parents of two different breeds or of unknown breeding. Mixed breeds are usually less expensive than purebreds.

If you want to buy a purebred horse, the seller must give you proof of the horse's breeding. A seller may say, "This is a purebred Welsh Pony," but unless you are an expert on Welsh Ponies, how can you be sure? A purebred horse will have "papers" from a breed registry. Papers are like a birth certificate and give the name of the horse's father (sire) and mother (dam).

A horse's breeding might be important to a professional trainer, but it's not really important in a first horse or pony. If a horse is suitable for you in other ways and the price is right, it doesn't matter who his parents were!

CONNEMARAS ARE NIMBLE JUMPERS.

PONY BREEDS

Ponies are small horses measuring up to 14.2 hands, and if you are not too tall, you can buy one to ride. Ponies tend to be hardy, and, if they are well fed and looked after properly, during cold weather many will grow thick, shaggy coats to keep them warm and can live outdoors happily. If you have a field that has some sort of shelter, like a run-in shed, you may not have to stable a pony at night in cool weather.

Here are three talented pony breeds you may come across in your search:

• The **Connemara Pony** is large and stands between 13 and 14.2 hh. These ponies are gentle and intelligent, and are great jumpers. The breed originated in Ireland.

WELSH PONIES ARE INTELLIGENT AND FRIENDLY.

CONNEMARAS ARE OFTEN DAPPLE GRAY.

A PONY OF THE AMERICAS IS COVERED WITH SPOTS!

- The **Welsh Pony** makes an excellent first pony. These ponies are bouncy jumpers and friendly to humans. They range from 12.2 to 15.2 hh— and they are very suitable for young people. The breed originated in Wales, a part of Great Britain.

APPALOOSAS ARE VERY COLORFUL.

- The **Pony of the Americas** is a very popular breed in the United States. The breed was developed over forty-one years ago when Appaloosa horses were crossed with high-quality ponies to produce talented, colorful mounts for young riders. These ponies have beautiful spotted coats, and because they are 46 to 56 inches high (11.5 to 14 hh), are perfectly sized for kids.

HORSE BREEDS

Horses are larger than ponies and stand 14.3 hh and over. If you are tall or have long legs, you may need to look for a horse instead of a pony. Horses aren't always as hardy as ponies, but depending on your climate, they can live outside year round if they have plenty of food and a shelter. Here are some breeds you might find in advertisements:

- The **Appaloosa** makes a great first horse. An Appaloosa's coat can be spotted or a solid color. This breed is used for everything: western riding, eventing, show jumping, hunting, and dressage. They are flashy looking, but sensible. If you touch an Appaloosa's spots, you can feel them!

- The **Morgan Horse** ranges in size from 14.2 to 15 hh. Morgans are reliable on the trail and can jump. Their high-stepping action makes them popular for dressage. Most Morgans can be handled easily by kids.

MORGANS ARE HIGH-STEPPERS. *(PHOTO: THE AMERICAN MORGAN HORSE ASSOCIATION; PHOTOGRAPHER: TERRI MILLER.)*

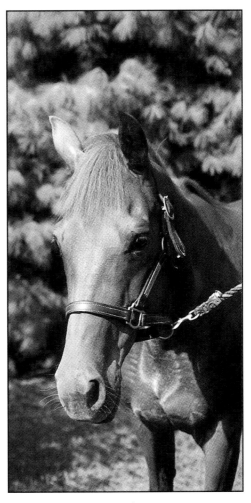

MORGANS ARE OFTEN CHESTNUT, BLACK, OR BAY.

QUARTER HORSES ARE MUSCULAR AND STRONG.

16 hh and can be any solid color.

- The **Arabian Horse** is very popular for both English and western riding. Arabians stand between 14.2 and 15.2 hh and only come in solid colors. These horses are very friendly and like people.

ARABIANS REALLY LIKE PEOPLE.

- A **Quarter Horse** may be your first choice if you want a strong and speedy horse. Quarter Horses are quick and nimble and can turn on a dime. They are usually between 15.1 and

If you live in a cold area, remember that Appaloosas, Quarter Horses, and Morgans can grow thick coats to keep them warm, but purebred Arabians rarely grow winter coats and may have to be kept in a stable during the cold season.

MIXED BREEDS

For a first horse, always choose a sensible mixed breed over a fancy purebred such as a Thoroughbred. Thoroughbreds are bred for racing and can be too high-strung to be suitable for children.

Some of the best ponies and horses are mixed breeds. For one thing, they are often hardier than purebred horses and ponies. They

SOME OF THE BEST FIRST HORSES ARE MIXED BREEDS.

tend to have fewer health problems and can stay out in a field in the winter unless it is extremely cold. If a pony is friendly and well behaved, it really doesn't matter what his breeding is!

5 Asking the Right Questions

Whoah! Don't gallop off right away and make an offer on a horse that sounds good in an ad. A horse may seem wonderful, but sellers aren't always as truthful as they should be. That's why you and your parents need to ask the seller some tough questions about the horse before you even hop in the car.

THE PHONE CALL

The next step in looking for a horse is making a phone call to the person advertising the horse for sale. If you are a teenager, you might feel confident enough to make the call yourself. If you are a bit younger, you should ask your mom or dad or your instructor to talk to the seller.

This important phone call will tell you whether or not a horse is worth visiting. There's no point in traveling two hours to discover that the horse that sounded perfect in the ad is a bucking bronco or costs twice as much as you can afford.

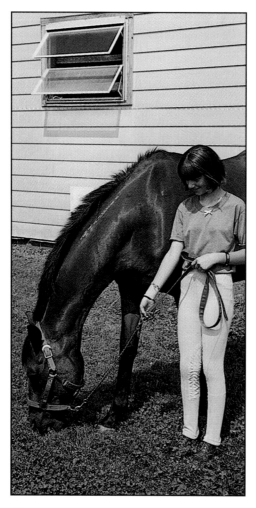

GATHER INFORMATION ABOUT A HORSE BEFORE YOU VISIT HIM.

Write the information you gather about the horse on a photocopy of the form on page 43. After you finish talking to the seller, you can discuss your notes with your parents or your instructor.

QUESTIONS TO ASK

✔ Is the horse or pony the right age, size, and price for you? Make sure the information in the ad is correct.

✔ How long has the seller owned the horse? If it has only been for a month or two, you should be suspicious. There might be a very good reason why the family is not keeping the horse. He might be dangerous or badly behaved, or have a physical problem, such as a sore back or bad feet.

✔ How long has the horse been for sale? If a horse is really good, he won't be for sale long because someone will snap him up quickly. Occasionally there are reasons for a slow sale. For example, a horse may be readvertised because a sale has fallen through due to "time-wasters," people who say they are going to buy the horse but then don't.

✔ What does the horse do best? Is he a talented jumper or a

✔ What sort of activities did the last rider do with the horse? If you want to jump, a horse that only does dressage is not for you. An all-rounder is one that will do flatwork one day, jump the next, and is happy to head out on a fun trail ride.

FIND OUT IF THE HORSE IS A GOOD JUMPER.

IS THE HORSE CALM ON TRAIL RIDES?

dressage horse? If you have a lot of money to spend on a horse, you can demand that he be a jumping or dressage star. But if you don't have a lot of money to spend, you'll have to be happy with a less fancy but totally reliable horse.

✔ Is the horse quiet enough for a beginner to ride and handle on his or her own? Even if you have been taking lessons at a riding school for several months, it is still best to buy a horse that is calm and obedient.

✔ Does he have any bad habits like biting, kicking, or bucking?

✔ Does the horse have any stable vices? "Stable vices" are annoying things a horse will do when he is bored. Cribbing is one of these. It means he chews on

IS THE HORSE QUIET ENOUGH FOR A BEGINNER TO HANDLE?

AVOID BUYING A HORSE THAT CRIBS OR EATS WOOD.

wood in his stable or on fences. Once a horse starts this habit, it is almost impossible to stop him from doing it. Cribbing is bad for a horse's stomach and can damage his teeth.

Another stable vice is weaving. This means a horse swings his head and neck from one side to the other over his stable door. He does it when he gets nervous or bored. Like cribbing, it is almost impossible to stop. Do not waste your time looking at a horse that cribs or weaves.

✔ Is the horse healthy? The owner should be able to tell you if the horse has ever had colic (a stomach ache) or been injured.

If an owner says that a horse was hurt but is now OK, you should still go to look at him. Some injuries heal perfectly and the horse can be fit and strong again. Don't pass up a horse with a scar or two.

✔ Has he competed in shows? A first horse should have been to

a show or two. If you are not very experienced yet, you don't want to have to deal with a nervous horse at his first show. You want a horse that has

ASK THE OWNER IF THE HORSE HAS BEEN TO SHOWS.

show experience so that you can concentrate on competing in your classes.

DON'T MAKE THESE MISTAKES IF YOU MAKE THE CALL

✔ Don't bother to ask all the questions if you find out early on that the horse isn't suitable. If he is too expensive or too inexperienced, you shouldn't waste the seller's time by asking lots of questions.

✔ Don't tell the owner how much money you are willing to pay for a horse. She might hike up the price if she thinks you have tons of money!

BE HONEST ABOUT YOUR RIDING ABILITY BEFORE YOU TRY A HORSE.

Is the horse easy to catch?

✔ Don't pretend you are a better rider than you are. Be honest about your riding ability, and let the owner know if you have never cantered or jumped. The minute you get on the horse, the seller will be able to tell how well you ride. If she has been expecting a member of the United States Equestrian Team, you could end up looking pretty silly!

✔ Don't phone without asking your parents or instructor first. They might set a limit on how far they are willing to travel to look at a horse. There's no point calling about a horse in California if you live in Florida.

ARRANGING A VISIT

If a horse sounds suitable to you, your parents, and your instructor, you can arrange to go see him. Fix a day and time, and get good directions.

Ask if the seller has a ring where you can try out the horse. If you are planning to jump the horse, it is important that the owner have a fence or two for you to pop over.

A SUITABLE HORSE WALKS INTO A TRAILER WITHOUT A FUSS.

Always ask an adult who knows about horses to go with you when you look at a horse. If your parents are not horse people, it is very important that you take your instructor or another knowledgeable person. You may have to pay that person for his or her time.

Phone Checklist

Make copies of this checklist and fill it out when you telephone a seller.

- ❏ Name of horse: _____
- ❏ Owner's name: _____
- ❏ Owner's telephone number: _____
- ❏ Location of horse: _____
- ❏ Price: _____
- ❏ Age: _____
- ❏ Sex: _____
- ❏ Size: _____
- ❏ How experienced is he? _____
- ❏ Can he jump? _____
- ❏ Has he been to any shows? _____
- ❏ Is he good on trails? _____
- ❏ Is he easy to catch? _____
- ❏ Is he good to shoe? _____
- ❏ Is he easy to load into a trailer? _____
- ❏ Is he healthy? _____
- ❏ Date and time of visit: _____

6 Trying a Horse

Always arrive on time when you go to look at a horse. Remember, the seller may want to show the horse to several people that day.

When you arrive at the stables, first impressions are important. The owner should be friendly and the barn should be tidy. The horse should be standing loose in his stall or out in his field. If he is tacked up, be suspicious. Ask if he has been ridden already that day and how many times. If a horse is frisky, someone could have ridden or lunged him to tire him out so that he'll behave quietly when you ride him.

The owner should have groomed the horse. If his coat is shaggy and covered with mud, it will be hard to tell what he really looks like.

A SUITABLE HORSE

Walk up to the horse and say hello. A good first horse pricks his ears when you walk up to him, and looks alert and friendly. He lets you catch him and halter him. He sniffs you to see if you have brought him a treat. He doesn't mind you patting him on his neck, shoulders, and back. He lets you pick up all four of his hooves.

A GOOD HORSE IS FRIENDLY AND LETS YOU PAT HIM.

A suitable horse looks healthy, well fed, and clean. His coat shines. Look at his hooves: they should be neatly trimmed and have no cracks. If he is wearing shoes, they should fit well and not have loose nails sticking out.

AN UNSUITABLE HORSE

A bad first horse turns away from you when you approach him. He is hard to catch. He shakes his head and throws it in the air so you have trouble putting on his halter. He looks grumpy and puts his ears back. He fidgets when you try to pick up his legs to pick out his hooves.

An unsuitable horse is skinny. You can see his ribs. His coat looks dirty. His hooves are cracked and uneven, and in need of a trim from the farrier.

Do not stick around if the owner seems scared of the horse.

A SUITABLE HORSE LETS YOU PICK UP HIS LEGS.

CONFORMATION

After you meet the horse, lead him out and look at his conformation. "Conformation" is the way a horse is put together and the way he looks. There are very few horses with a perfect

LOOK AT THE HORSE'S LEGS. ARE THEY NICE AND STRAIGHT?

If the horse's owner is a child but an adult does all the work for her, like tacking up or grooming, it might mean that the horse is nasty to kids. Better to be extra suspicious now before you buy the horse, rather than sorry afterwards when you bring the little devil home!

47

DOES THE HORSE WEAR REGULAR SHOES LIKE THESE?

conformation. Perhaps you have seen a horse with a big head or a thin neck.

Some kinds of poor conformation only affect the way a horse looks. They don't affect his performance. For example, a horse might have big funny ears, but huge ears won't stop him from jumping. But other conformation problems may be signs of a physical weakness and could affect the

way the horse moves. If he has crooked legs, he might not be able to canter properly, and he could get lame a lot.

Here are some basic conformation points to check for when looking at a possible purchase:

- All four of the horse's legs should be straight, not knock-kneed, which means his knees bend inward. If his hooves point inward he is pigeon-toed. If they point outward he is splayfooted. If his back legs bend in, he is cow-hocked. If they bend out he is bow-legged. These faults could (but might not) affect how he walks, trots, canters, and jumps.

- His hooves should be in good condition—no cracks or rough edges. They should be hard. All four feet should be the same size and shape. If his shoes are unusually shaped, you should ask why. Special shoes may mean that he has a weakness in his hooves or legs.

- Are his legs smooth or covered with bumps? If a horse has any large lumps or scars, ask how he got them. Bumps can be splints. "Splints" are bony growths on a horse's leg that are sometimes caused by too much work at a young age. Only a vet can tell if splints will cause problems.

- A horse's back should dip slightly in the middle but not

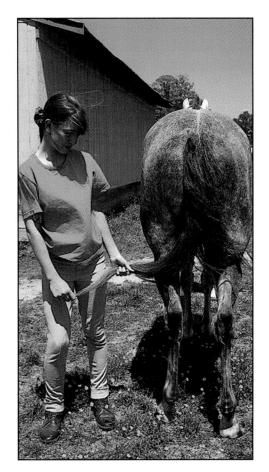

HIS BACK LEGS SHOULD NOT BEND IN TOO MUCH.

too much. If it dips down too much he has a 'sway back' and it might be hard to find a saddle that fits him.

- His withers, the bony base of a horse's neck where the mane

CHECK THOSE LEGS FOR LUMPS AND BUMPS!

starts, should not stick up too much because it will be hard to find a saddle that fits properly.

TESTING ON THE GROUND

Now that you have checked the conformation of the horse, it's time to see how he moves and behaves, but don't get on him yet.

Here are some things you should do when handling a horse for the first time:

- Lead the horse in his halter with a lead rope. If he pulls you around or barges in front of you, or refuses to move at all, he probably has bad manners.

- Tie the horse up. He should stand pretty still and should not back up or try to break the lead rope.

50

- Give the horse a quick grooming. He should not try to nip or kick you as you brush him.

- Find out what sort of feed the horse eats. Does he have a special diet because of a delicate stomach? You don't want to have to pay extra money for special feed for a fussy eater.

- Look at the horse's stable and the bedding on the floor. Is it straw or wood shavings? Sometimes a horse will have special dust-free bedding, such as shredded paper, because he has a breathing problem or an allergy caused by straw. Think twice before buying a horse with a breathing problem or an allergy.

OFFER TO HELP GROOM THE HORSE.

51

ASK IF YOU CAN TACK UP THE HORSE BY YOURSELF.

LEAD THE HORSE IN HIS HALTER WITH A LEAD ROPE.

- Find out if he will he load into a trailer.

- Ask the owner if you can help tack up the horse. The horse should stand quietly as you put on his saddle and bridle.

TACK

Look at his tack carefully. A first horse should be ridden safely in a bridle with a simple snaffle bit and plain noseband. A martingale is OK, too. Steer clear of a horse wearing a severe bit like a

THE HORSE SHOULD WEAR A SIMPLE SNAFFLE BIT LIKE THIS ONE.

gag, a figure-eight noseband, or other gadgets. These could mean that the horse is very strong and difficult to stop or turn. Your instructor should be able to spot extra-strong bits or nosebands and warn you about them.

WATCH CLOSELY

Never, ever ride a horse right away. The owner should have

another child or person ride the horse in front of you and your parents and instructor. Here are some things to watch for:

- **Spurs or whips** Is the rider wearing spurs on her boots or carrying a whip? Watch how she uses them. If she kicks the horse continually with the spurs, or hits him frequently with the whip, he may not be the perfect horse for you. He may be

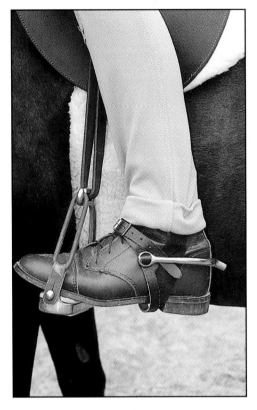

A FIRST HORSE SHOULDN'T NEED SPURS.

DOES HE STAND STILL WHEN HE IS MOUNTED?

stubborn and too lazy to be a good first horse.

If you haven't used a whip before, don't carry one when you try the horse. It will only get in your way. Don't reject a horse just because his rider carries a whip. A horse that is a little bit lazy can often be a terrific first horse.

- **Mounting** Does the horse stand quietly, or does he move around and try to bite the rider? Does she cling tightly to the reins so that he won't move, or does he stand still on a loose rein?

- **Walking on a loose rein** Ask the rider to walk around the arena on a loose rein at first.

Does the horse walk forward freely, or does he look tense? Look at the rider's feet. If she is kicking the horse a lot, he may be ignoring her instructions.

- **Trot and canter** The rider should pick up the reins and ask the horse to trot. Watch him trot in both directions around the arena. He should not rush around at top speed, nor should he move along slowly with his nose on the ground. A horse should not throw his head up in the air, either.

Watch the horse canter in both directions. Does he pick up both leads easily? Does he gallop off with the rider, or does he canter steadily?

- **Halt and stand still** A first horse must halt and stand still when he is asked. The rider should not have to tug on the reins.

- **Jumping** If you plan to jump your new horse when you get home, watch him jump a couple of fences at a trot and

WATCH CLOSELY AS THE HORSE WALKS AROUND THE ARENA.

THE HORSE SHOULD CANTER STEADILY.

ASK THE OWNER TO JUMP THE HORSE OVER A FENCE OR TWO.

canter. Does he rush toward the jumps like a maniac or approach them sensibly? He should look straight ahead at the fence and not throw his head to one side.

If he knocks one or two fences down, don't worry about it. If he knocks down every single fence, you'd better not buy him!

YOUR TURN!

After you have seen the horse put through his paces by someone else, you can try him out yourself. Put on your safety helmet and hop on. It's possible you will feel a bit nervous. It's difficult to ride a horse you've never met before—especially if lots of people are watching you.

Walk the horse around the arena a couple of times. Get used to him. When you feel ready, pick up a trot. Trot some circles and straight lines. Does the horse respond to your legs and hands, or does he ignore you? Check that you can stop him from both

EVERY HORSE SHOULD HALT WHEN HE IS ASKED.

NOW IT'S YOUR TURN TO TRY HIM OUT!

ASK YOUR INSTRUCTOR TO GIVE YOU A MINI LESSON.

DOES HE FEEL BUMPY AT THE TROT?

a walk and a trot before you canter.

Canter in some small circles, then go all around the arena. Is it easy to get him to move forward? Can you keep him cantering all around the ring? Your legs will

CANTER AROUND THE ARENA A COUPLE OF TIMES.

HE SHOULD WALK BRISKLY BY THE ARENA GATE.

soon get tired if you have to kick, kick, kick all the time!

On the other hand, is he too zippy for you? Does the slightest nudge of your legs make him gallop off with you around the ring? If a horse scares you or if you have trouble slowing him down, do not buy him.

Does the horse slow down near the arena gate? If he does, he might be barn sour. This means the horse spends most of his time thinking about how he

IT SHOULD BE EASY TO GET THE HORSE TO HALT.

SHORTEN YOUR STIRRUPS BEFORE YOU POP OVER A FENCE.

can get out of work and back to his stable!

Finally, ask the horse to halt. He should stop when you ask him.

POP OVER A FENCE

Your instructor may want you to jump. Raise your stirrups a hole or two and pop over a small cross-pole fence at a trot.

Do you feel scared jumping the horse, or is it fun? Is he comfortable to jump, or does he throw you five feet out of the saddle? If the horse tosses his head up and rushes the fence at top speed, don't buy him. A speed demon that crashes through fences will scare you and ruin your confidence.

Ask your instructor or parents to set up a small course of three or four fences and jump them all. The horse should jump them at a steady speed.

59

JUMPING THE HORSE SHOULD BE FUN!

Don't worry if he refuses a jump or two. You don't know each other very well and a refusal is understandable. The horse is used to another rider—not you!

ROAD SENSE

If you plan to ride your new horse on or near roads, he must be used to cars and trucks. Ask the owner if the horse is afraid of traffic. It could be dangerous if the horse is frightened of cars and bolts when he spots one coming close.

See if the owner will let you walk down the road with the horse while your instructor walks alongside you.

MAKING A DECISION

Don't waste time if you don't like the horse. If you can tell even

COULD YOU STOP HIM EASILY?

TALK TO YOUR INSTRUCTOR AND YOUR PARENTS BEFORE DECIDING TO BUY A HORSE.

before riding him that he will be too much for you to handle, say thank you and leave. Too many kids make the mistake of buying the first horse they try.

If you like the horse and feel safe on him, don't offer the owner a deposit right away. You, your parents, and your instructor should spend a few minutes in private discussing the horse. What do your parents think? Does your instructor like the horse?

WAS THE HORSE EASY TO TACK UP?

61

Some owners may let you take a horse on trial. This means you can take him home and try him out for a week or two.

Most sellers will bargain a bit over the price and many will settle for a slightly lower amount than advertised. But if a seller has several people who want the horse, she may demand the full price.

Make copies of this checklist and fill it out after you have seen a horse. It will help you make a decision about him.

❏ What sort of personality does the horse have?

Friendly? Grumpy?

❏ How are his stable manners? Does he bite or barge around?

❏ Does he look healthy and well cared for?

❏ How does he like other horses? Does he kick?

❏ Is he well behaved when he is groomed?

❏ Does he stand still when he is tacked up?

❏ What sort of tack does he wear?

   Bridle: Bit: Any gadgets:

❏ Does he stand still when you are mounting?

❏ Is he the right size for you?

❏ How is he at the walk?

❏ How is he at the trot?

❏ How is he at the canter?

❏ Does he like to jump?

❏ How is he in traffic?

❏ Will he load into a trailer?

Pre-Purchase Vetting

You can't tell by looking at a horse that he has something wrong with him—that's a vet's job. After you hand over a deposit on the horse you have chosen, you must arrange for a veterinarian to give him a pre-purchase exam.

Paying a vet to look at the horse before you buy him might save you money later on if you find out that he is lame, has a breathing problem, or has some other defect. A small bump on a horse's leg might turn out to be a splint, which could cause lameness in a year or two. A runny nose could mean the horse has an allergy, which could stop him from doing hard work.

Ask your riding instructor if she knows a good horse veterinarian who can do the exam. If she can't recommend one, call a local riding school and see whom the manager recommends.

Next, call up the horse's owner and arrange a time when the vet can come to examine the horse. It should be during daylight hours so the vet can get a good look at the horse. Then call the vet and set up an appointment.

You and your parents should be present when the vet gives the horse a pre-purchase exam. It usually takes about an hour and a half. Bring riding clothes and a helmet in case the vet asks you to ride the horse.

OPEN WIDE! THE VET EXAMINES THE HORSE'S TEETH.

Here are some of the things a vet will do:

- Looks at the horse's teeth. A vet will be able to tell how old the horse is if he is under nine. If he is over nine, she can still make a pretty good guess about his age.

  The vet checks to see if the horse's teeth are in good condition. She will be able to tell if he cribs (chews on wood), because if he does, his teeth will be worn down. If the teeth are too long or too sharp in places, it might mean that the horse cannot eat his food properly and will have a problem keeping on weight.

- Looks down the horse's throat and up his nose to make sure they are clean and free of any obstructions.

• Looks into the horse's eyes through an instrument called an ophthalmoscope. The opthalmoscope has a light beam that the vet shines into the horse's eyes.

She may discover a cataract, an eye ailment that usually affects older horses. This means that the lens of the eye, which should be clear, is turning white and will prevent the horse from seeing clearly. Don't buy a horse with cataracts, because his vision might get worse.

• Looks in the horse's ears. Ears are perfect homes for lice and mites, which are small bugs. Mites irritate a horse. He'll shake his head a lot and rub his ears. The vet also checks to make sure the horse doesn't have a build-up of ear wax. This is not serious, because wax can be broken down with ear drops.

• Listens to the horse's heart and lungs with a stethoscope while

THE VET CHECKS THE HORSE'S EYES.

he is standing quietly. The vet will be able to tell if the heart is beating normally and if the lungs are clear of fluids so that the horse can breathe easily.

• Feels for swellings, lumps, or scars on the horse's body. If the horse has lumps on his legs, the

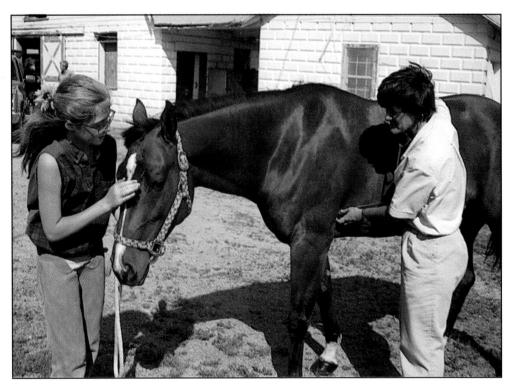

The vet listens to the horse's heart and lungs.

vet will tell you if they are from old injuries that could cause lameness later on, or if they are not serious.

She picks up the horse's legs to make sure his knee and hock joints are flexible and working well. She inspects his hooves, too.

• Watches the horse (wearing only a halter and lead rope) walk and trot in hand. The vet does this to see if she can spot lameness. She picks up each one of the horse's legs and twists it a bit, puts it down, then asks the horse to trot away from her quickly. This is called a flexion test. If the horse has a problem trotting, it could mean he has joint trouble and might become lame.

ARE THE HORSE'S HOOVES IN GOOD SHAPE?

• Watches the horse being ridden or lunged. The vet observes the horse as he walks and trots. Then she asks for the horse to be cantered for several minutes.

The vet listens to the horse's breathing as he canters in a circle around her. Raspy breathing or grunting could mean the horse has lung problems. After the horse canters, the vet

THE VET WATCHES THE HORSE TROT.

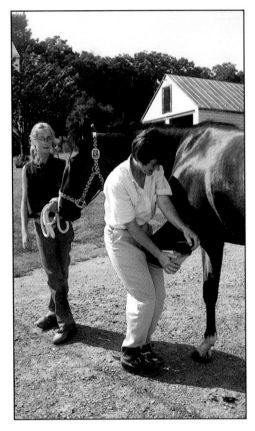

THE VET DOES THE FLEXION TEST TO SEE IF THE HORSE IS LAME.

dangerous viruses that might spread to other horses.

After the inspection, the vet fills out a certificate. She writes down the horse's age and notes all of his markings for identification. Then the vet tells you if the horse has passed or failed the examination. If the horse passes

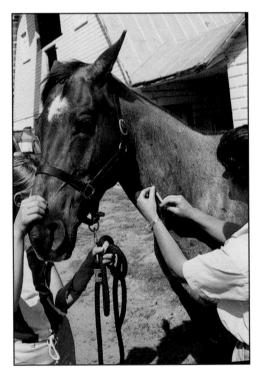

THE VET TAKES A BLOOD SAMPLE TO TEST FOR VIRUSES.

listens to his breathing again. To see how fit he is, she notes how long it takes for the horse's breathing to slow down after hard exercise.

• Takes a blood sample and tests it to see if the horse has any

YOU MAY HAVE TO RIDE THE HORSE FOR THE VET.

the veterinary inspection, you can buy him!

If he fails, ask why. The vet may tell you that the horse has a problem that can be cured with treatment. She may tell you that the horse has a permanent problem that can be managed with special care, although it will never go away. You and your parents may decide that this is all right with you and that you want to buy the horse anyway.

The vet may say that the horse has a serious flaw. If she thinks the horse is unsuitable for you, she's probably right. Even though it might be hard, you must say goodbye to the horse and keep searching for a new four-legged friend.

8 Taking Your New Horse Home

If you are lucky enough to live on a farm or own several acres of land, you may have a ready-made home for your new horse. Otherwise, you will have to find somewhere to keep him. Your horse's new home should not be too far away from your house. Remember, your parents will have to drive you to the barn and they won't want to travel 60 miles each way! Make sure they understand that you should visit your horse every day.

Your instructor may know of a good place to keep your horse, or you could look in the Yellow Pages under "horses" or "stables" for a home for him. Check the local tack shop bulletin board, too. Here are some of the homes you and your parents might choose for your new horse.

A BOARDING BARN

You could keep your horse at a boarding barn. This may be just a farm with fields and stables, but good boarding barns have riding rings, too. A barn has a manager and a staff who feed your horse every day and make sure that he is healthy and happy.

YOU COULD KEEP YOUR HORSE AT A BOARDING BARN.

YOU'LL MAKE PONY PALS AT A RIDING SCHOOL.

A boarding barn is a great place for a first-time horse owner. A lot of people will be around to help you and to explain horsey things to you. Find out if other children board their horses there so you can make some pony pals.

A RIDING SCHOOL

Keeping your new horse at a riding school is a good idea. There will be lots of kids to ride with and you can take lessons. Schools

IF YOU LET YOUR HORSE BE RIDDEN IN LESSONS, YOUR BOARD WILL BE CHEAPER.

often have rings and jumps you can use.

Some schools will give you a discount if you let them use your horse in lessons a few times a week. If you decide to do this, your parents will have to talk to the manager first. They must find out how much your pony will be used, who will ride him, and who is responsible if he gets hurt.

YOUR OWN FARM

If you plan to keep your horse at home, you must have a field or

YOUR HORSE SHOULD HAVE PLENTY OF GRASS.

FIND OUT WHAT YOUR HORSE EATS BEFORE YOU BRING HIM HOME.

a shelter or a stable in case he gets sick and needs to be inside.

Your horse should have some equine company. Horses are herd animals and don't like being alone. Each horse should also have at least one acre of grazing.

Before you take your horse home, find out his daily routine,

YOUR NEW HORSE NEEDS SOME EQUINE COMPANY.

pasture with a strong fence. There should be no barbed wire that could injure a horse, and there must be grass for him to nibble, trees to give him some shade on hot days, and a constant water supply. Even if your horse will stay out all the time, he still needs

and what and when he is fed. Knowing his regular schedule and sticking to it will make his move to his new home easier.

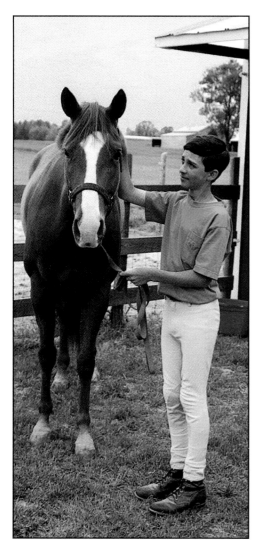

FINALLY, HE'S ALL YOURS!

BUY OR BORROW SHIPPING BOOTS FOR YOUR HORSE.

CHECK, PLEASE

Once the vet has given the horse the OK, you will have to pay for him. By now, your parents and the seller should have agreed on a price.

Ready to roll!

The seller will tell your parents whether she wants cash, a check, or a certified bank check. Your parents can pay when you pick up the horse. Ask the seller for a signed receipt naming you or your parents as the owner of the horse.

If the horse is a purebred, the seller should give you his registration papers. As the new owner, you must re-register the horse with the breed association. The seller should also give you the horse's veterinary records.

INSURANCE

The moment a horse becomes your property, it's a good idea to cover him with some sort of insurance policy. You pay an insurance company a fee each year and, in return, if your horse is stolen, needs medical attention, or is

FRESH HAY IN A HAY NET GIVES YOUR HORSE SOMETHING TO MUNCH ON IN THE TRAILER.

involved in an accident, the company will cover some or all of the costs that pop up. Some insurance policies will even pay for your medical treatment if you fall off your horse and hurt yourself.

Your parents can ask their own insurance agent for a horse policy or they can look in horse magazines for insurance ads.

You will have to fill out a form describing the horse and what sort of activities you are planning to do with him, for example, showing or trail riding. If you will be doing something more risky, like show jumping or eventing (jumping big fences cross-country), the insurance policy may cost more. You may also have to show the insurance agent a copy of the horse's veterinary records. Most companies want to make sure the horse is fit as a fiddle before he is insured.

ON THE ROAD

You will need a horse trailer to get your horse to his new home. There's no problem if you have your own trailer and one of your parents is an experienced driver who has pulled a trailer before.

WALK YOUR HORSE AROUND HIS NEW HOME.

If you don't have a trailer, don't go out and borrow one if neither of your parents has ever pulled one before. Learning to pull a trailer takes practice. Ask your instructor if she will pick up the horse for you.

Borrow or buy protective shipping boots and put them on your horse before he gets in the trailer. Shipping boots are padded boots that protect a horse's legs so he won't hurt them if he falls or gets bumped in the trailer. Your horse should also wear a head protector.

Make sure there is a hay net in the trailer so the horse has some fresh hay to munch on during the journey. It helps to keep him happy and quiet.

WELCOME HOME!

When you arrive at your barn, walk your new horse around so he can have a good look at everything.

If your horse is going to live in a field with other horses, it's not a good idea to put him in with the

TURN YOUR HORSE OUT BY HIMSELF AT FIRST.

others right away. Horses live in herds, and each herd has its own "pecking order." This means that in each herd there is one horse who is the boss. The boss usually gets fed first and will bully younger or new horses. Your horse may get picked on.

Once you put your horse out in the field with a group of horses, they will zoom around like mad. There will be lots of squealing and bucking, and it will be

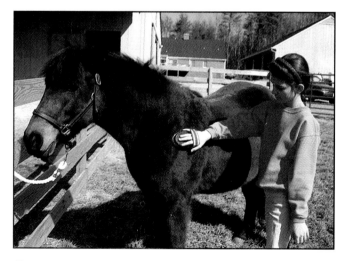

GET TO KNOW YOUR HORSE BY GROOMING HIM.

nerve-wracking! Watch to make sure your new horse does not get hurt. He may get bitten or kicked if he is unlucky, but mostly he and the other horses will try to get to know each other. Eventually the herd will get bored and leave him alone.

Keep your horse's halter on for the first day or two so you can catch him easily.

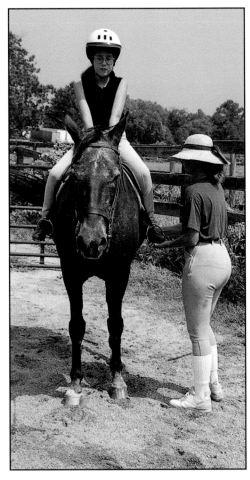

HAVE A LESSON ON YOUR NEW FRIEND.

RIDING YOUR NEW HORSE

Don't jump onto your horse the minute he arrives at your barn. He needs time to settle in before you ride him. He needs to get used to

HE'LL APPRECIATE A TASTY TREAT OR TWO!

his new schedule and his new horsey friends. Riding him right away may upset him. He may misbehave because he is nervous.

Give him a week to settle in. Use this time to get to know him. Spend time grooming or feeding him. It won't be long before he knows who you are—especially if you bring him snacks of carrots or apples.

When you ride him for the first time, don't gallop along trails at top speed. Take it easy. You don't know each other very well yet. Stick to a ring for your first few rides, and have a lesson with your instructor so she can see how you and your horse are getting along.

The first time you go out on a trail, follow a friend. You don't know how your horse is going to behave, so it's best to have someone along who can help you if you have problems.

HAVE COMPANY ON YOUR FIRST TRAIL RIDE.

American Camping
Association
800-777-CAMP

American Connemara
Pony Society
2630 Hunting Ridge Road
Winchester, VA 22603
540-662-5953

American Horse Council
1700 K Street NW
Suite 300
Washington, DC 20006-3805
202-296-4031

American Horse Shows
Association
220 East 42nd Street
Suite 409
New York, NY 10017
212-972-2472

American Morgan Horse
Association
P.O. Box 960
Shelburne, VT 05482-0960
802-985-4944

American Quarter Horse
Association
P.O. Box 200
Amarillo, TX 79168
806-376-4811

American Riding Instructors
Association
P.O. Box 282
Alton Bay, NH 03810-0282
603-875-4000

American Quarter Horse
Association
P.O. Box 200
Amarillo, TX 79168-0001
806-376-4811

Useful Addresses

American Youth Horse Council
4193 Iron Works Pike
Lexington, KY 40511-2742
800-TRY-AYHC

Appaloosa Horse Club, Inc.
P.O. Box 8403
Moscow, ID 83843-0903
208-882-5578

**Arabian Horse Registry
of America**
12000 Zuni Street
Westminster, CO 80234-2300
303-450-4748

Canadian Pony Club
National Office
6th Floor
1 Rideau Street
Ottawa KIN 8S7, Canada
613-241-7429

**CHA—The Association for
Horsemanship Safety and
Education**
5318 Old Bullard Road
Tyler, TX 75703
800-399-0138

Future Farmers of America
P.O. Box 15160
Alexandria, VA 22309
703-360-3600

National 4-H Council
7100 Connecticut Avenue
Chevy Chase, MD 20815-4999
301-961-2830

**North American Riding for the
Handicapped Association
(NARHA)**
P.O. Box 33150
Denver, CO 80233
800-369-RIDE (7433)
    or 303-452-1212

Pony of the Americas Club
5240 Elmwood Avenue
Indianapolis, IN 46203-5990
317-788-0107

The United States Pony Clubs
4071 Iron Works Pike
Lexington, KY 40511-8462
606-254-PONY (7669)

**Welsh Pony and Cob Society
of America**
P.O. Box 2977
Winchester, VA 22604-2977
703-667-6195

I would like to thank the following people and organizations for their help with this book:

Katherine and Susan Waldrop; Betsy Daniel and the students at James River Riding School, Richmond, Virginia; Rachel and Shayla Saltz; Celia Geotzl and Melinda Cohen; Samra Zelman and Rebecca Yount; Amy Marcum; Eric and Betty Mathews; Amanda Davis; Katherine Foley; Allison Wendling; Annette Slowinski, DVM; Paula Grimstead, Farrier; Jenny and Michelle Smith; Jamie and Marlene Blackburn; Natasha Damien; Kate and Kay Sammons; Laura Crews; Level Green Riding School, Powhatan, Virginia; Aynsley Wilton; Megan Tubbs; Erin Keck; Erin King; Sarah Lepley; Sonia Bennett; Heather King; Barrett Wright; Michelle Rudick; and Richmond Saddlery.

Acknowledgments